JOSEPH'S COAT OF MANY COLORS

Louis Weber, C.E.O.
Publications International, Ltd.
7373 North Cicero Avenue
Lincolnwood, Illinois 60646

Manufactured in USA.

8 7 6 5 4 3 2 I

ISBN: 1-56173-721-6

Contributing Writer: Marlene Targ Brill

Consultant: David M. Howard, Jr., Ph.D.

Cover Illustration: Stephen Marchesi

Book Illustrations: Gary Torrisi

David M. Howard, Jr., Ph.D. is an associate professor of Old Testament
and Semitic Languages, and is a member of the Society of Biblical
Literature and the Institute for Biblical Research.

Publications International, Ltd.

Long ago, in the land of Canaan, lived a man named Jacob. He had many animals. He also had many children. Of all his children, Jacob loved Joseph best. To show his love, Jacob made a bright and colorful robe. Then he gave it to his favorite son.

Joseph had ten older brothers. When they found out that their father had given Joseph this special gift, they became jealous. Later, Joseph had two dreams. When he told his brothers about the dreams, they became even more upset. Joseph said the dreams showed that his brothers would some day bow down to him. "You think your dreams mean you will rule over us," his brothers said angrily.

Soon after Joseph's dreams, the brothers had to go to take care of the animals in the fields. They were gone for a long time. Jacob told Joseph, "Go and see if your brothers and the flock are okay. Then come back and tell me what you heard."

When the brothers saw Joseph walking toward them, they saw he was wearing his special robe. They got angry all over again.

When Joseph reached them, they ripped off his robe. They threw him into an empty pit and sat down to eat. A group of traders passed by their flock. One brother said, "Let's sell our brother to these traders. We will get money, and he will live."

The brothers pulled Joseph out of the pit. They sold their brother to the traders for money. But what would they tell their father? They killed a goat and dipped the coat into the blood. Then they took the coat to their father.

"It is my son's coat," Jacob cried. "A wild animal must have killed him." Jacob wept and wept. He was so sad, nothing could make him feel better.

Meanwhile, Joseph had been sold as a slave in Egypt. But God was watching over him. A court official named Potiphar bought Joseph and put him in charge of all he owned. Then one day Joseph was blamed for something he didn't do. But Potiphar did not believe Joseph.

In fact, Potiphar was so angry, he had Joseph thrown into the pharaoh's prison. Joseph shared a cell with two men who had been the pharaoh's baker and chief cupbearer.

During that time, the cupbearer had a dream. Joseph explained it to him. What Joseph said came true. Soon, Pharaoh forgave the cupbearer and returned him to his palace job.

Joseph spent two more years in jail. But God took care of him there. One night, Pharaoh had two dreams that troubled him. But there was no one in Egypt who could explain the dreams. Finally, the cupbearer remembered Joseph. He told Pharaoh about the young man who was able to explain what dreams mean.

Pharaoh sent for Joseph and had him listen to the dreams. "Both dreams mean the same thing, Pharaoh," Joseph said. "God told you what will happen. There will be seven good years. Crops will grow and food will be plentiful. Then there will be seven bad years. The land will be dry and no food will grow. Everyone will be very hungry."

Joseph suggested that Pharaoh select a wise man to collect food during the good years. The stored food would feed the people of Egypt during the bad years. Pharaoh liked the plan, so he put Joseph in charge. He ordered people to bow down to Joseph. Now only Pharaoh was greater among the people than Joseph.

Everything happened just as Joseph had said it would. During the next seven years, there was a wealth of crops. Joseph had the food gathered and stored. Then the seven years of plenty ended. During the next seven years, no food grew. People cried from hunger in every country. But there was bread throughout Egypt.

"Go to Joseph," Pharaoh told his people. "Do what he says." Joseph opened the filled and overflowing storehouses. He sold bread to people from all over the world.

Back in Canaan, Jacob and his family needed food, too. He sent his sons to Egypt to buy bread. But Jacob kept his youngest son, Benjamin, at home. He was afraid something bad might happen to him.

The brothers came to Joseph and bowed down. They did not recognize him, but Joseph recognized them! He pretended not to know them and asked who they were. "We are honest men from Canaan. We are twelve sons of one man. The youngest is with our father. One brother is no more."

Joseph had a plan. He said they were spies and sent them to prison for three days. When they were allowed to go home, Joseph said they had to leave one brother, Simeon, in Egypt. They were to bring Benjamin back to prove they were telling the truth.

Joseph had the money they used to buy grain put inside the bags. On the way home, they found the money. They were sure they would get in trouble!

When they got home, they told Jacob what happened. Jacob did not want to let Benjamin go back with them. But when the grain was gone, Jacob realized he had to let Benjamin go.

The brothers returned to Joseph. When he saw Benjamin, Joseph had to leave the room. He was happy and sad at the same time. They ate dinner and Joseph had the sacks of grain prepared. The servants put the money in them like before. But this time he had them hide a silver cup in Benjamin's sack.

The brothers started on their way home. Joseph sent guards to catch up with them. They told them that someone had stolen a silver cup. The brothers said, "We would never do that."

The guards searched the sacks. There was the silver cup! They took the brothers back to Joseph. The brothers fell to the ground before Joseph and begged him to let them go. Joseph agreed to let everyone go—everyone except Benjamin. Since the cup was in his sack, he was to stay as Joseph's servant.

"The boy's father will die without him," cried the brothers. Joseph couldn't keep the secret any longer. He told them who he was.

"Do not worry," Joseph told his troubled brothers. "It was God, not you, who sent me here. God made me Pharaoh's ruler over all the land to keep you alive." Joseph hugged Benjamin and wept. He kissed all his brothers.

Pharaoh told Joseph to move the whole family to Egypt. The Pharaoh said, "I will give you the best land."

Everyone in Jacob's family came to Egypt. Joseph greeted them. Jacob and Joseph were very happy to see each other again.